100 Days

100 Days

Copyright © Glenn Myers 2002

First published in 2002 by Authentic Lifestyle
08 07 06 05 04 03 02   7 6 5 4 3 2 1

Authentic Lifestyle is an imprint of Authentic Media
PO Box 300, Carlisle, Cumbria, CA3 0QS, UK, and
Box 1047, Waynesboro, GA 30830-2047, USA
www.paternoster-publishing.com

Glenn Myers has asserted his right under the Copyright, Designs and Patents Act 1988 to be
identified as the Author of this work which is based on the 2001 edition of 'Operation World'
by Patrick Johnstone and Jason Mandryk

British Library Cataloguing in Publication Data
A catalogue record is available from the British Library   ISBN: 1-85078-428-0

Scripture quotations from the Holy Bible New International Version® NIV® Used by permission of
Zondervan Publishing House. All rights reserved © 1973, 1978, 1984 by International Bible Society

Cover design by Campsie
Printed by Interprint Limited, Malta

This book is produced by WEC International
WEC is an interdenominational missions agency that introduces the Christian
gospel to people around the world who have yet to hear or experience it. WEC
has over 2,000 workers from about 50 nations serving together in 60 countries.
www.wec-int.org

100 Days

100 days of prayer for the world
from *Operation World*

Compiled by Glenn Myers
Design and supplementary material: Dave Davidson and Glenn Myers

Operation World

21st Century Edition

The definitive prayer guide to the nations, peoples and cities of the world

- Completely updated and revised – the first time for eight years

- Key background information for every country

- Major prayer challenges gathered direct from hundreds of on-site Christian workers across all denominations

- Answers to prayer carefully logged (new for this edition)

- Complete with all-new maps, cross-references, addresses and indexes

- The most comprehensive, up-to-date and wide-ranging compilation of prayer information ever produced

ISBN 1-85078-357-8

www.operationworld.org

WHEN WE PRAY GOD WORKS

I urge, then, first of all, that requests, **prayers, intercession** and thanksgiving be made for everyone ...

This is good, and pleases God our Saviour who **wants all men to be saved** and come to a knowledge of the truth. 1 Timothy 2:1-4

Pray in the Spirit on all occasions with **all kinds of prayers** and requests. With this in mind be alert and **always keep on praying** for all the saints. Ephesians 6:18

Azerbaijan (Eurasia)

○ ○ ○ ○ ○ ○ ○ ○ ○ ○ ○ ○ ○ ○ ○

Azerbaijan's political situation is complex and potentially dangerous … unresolved conflict with Armenia.

Pray for peace with a just resolution

Christianity is associated with Russian imperialism and Armenian occupation … Possibly 2000 Azeri believers in the country …

Most Azerbaijani towns and villages have never been evangelized

Who shall separate us from the love of Christ? Shall trouble or hardship or persecution or famine or nakedness or danger or sword? Romans 8:35

Armenia (Eurasia)

O O O O O O O O O O O O O O O

The world's first Christian nation
70 years of Marxism and a century of severe
persecution have left deep moral and social wounds

The Armenian Apostolic Church has long been a cultural
refuge in times of persecution. The 1988 earthquake helped
to bring about a powerful revival with national repentance

before the Lord

Pray for:
a complete recovery from division and compromise;
deep spiritual regeneration of the Church
and fellowship with smaller denominations

DAY 1

South Africa

○ ○ ○ ○ ○ ○ ○ ○ ○ ○ ○ ○ ○ ○ ○

Strenuous efforts by local churches to roll back the centuries of oppression have borne fruit; need for *ongoing healing* and

reconciliation

Escalating crime: **murder rate** over seven times that of the USA. AIDS, the primary cause of death, affects over 20% of adults and one third of all teachers.

Biblical Christianity
continues to thrive

... prayer networks, evangelism, missions, social concern ...
despite the post-Christian moral slide

Tibet (China)

○ ○ ○ ○ ○ ○ ○ ○ ○ ○ ○ ○ ○ ○ ○

The Communists have systematically

sought to destroy

the culture, religions and ethnic identity
of the Tibetan people … frequent revolts …

Over one million people may have lost

their

lives

Tibetan Buddhism has a strong hold on the people …
After centuries of failed attempts there may be about
1,000 evangelical and 2,000 Catholic Christians among
the 5m Tibetans in the world.

DAY 2

**For the Son of Man came to seek
and to save what was lost.** Luke 19:10

Morocco and Western Sahara

(Arab world)

O O O O O O O O O O O O O O O

Morocco: 'Freedom of religion' but no freedom to leave Islam ...
A widespread and growing interest in the gospel ...
A Church is emerging, maybe 500 believers by 2000, but at great
cost.

Great expectations

for democracy, the economy, and the underprivileged
through the new King's efforts

Western Sahara: 70% of the land, invaded by Morocco,
is guarded behind a 1500 km-long earthen wall.
On the other side is Polisario, a liberation movement.
Almost no Christians on either side.

I eagerly expect and hope that I will in no way be ashamed,
but will have sufficient courage so that now as always Christ will
be exalted in my body, whether by life or by death. Philippians 1:20

New Zealand

○ ○ ○ ○ ○ ○ ○ ○ ○ ○ ○ ○ ○ ○ ○ ○

Church attendance is declining … a growing interest in New Age religions. Earlier Pentecostal and charismatic growth has slowed.

Pray for a fresh outpouring of the Spirit

Large communities of Pacific Islanders live in the cities, often in poorer areas where crime is high. Many go to church but young people are generally disillusioned with their churches.

DAY 3

Mexico (Latin America)

Dynamic, growing nation … most Mexicans are culturally Catholic, but only 10% are regular churchgoers.

Pray that the power of the ancient gods and spirit-world may be broken

Evangelicals have grown…

now perhaps 7% of the population. This growth has disturbed the conservative wing of the Catholic Church.

Pray that Evangelical growth may stimulate reform and renewal rather than persecution. Pray that the believers will demonstrate the meekness and love of their Saviour.

Europe's small countries

o o o o o o o o o o o o o o o o

Materialism holds *Andorra* in a tight grip.
The occult is a stronghold in this beautiful principality.

Almost the entire indigenous population is Catholic
(Liechtenstein, Monaco).

San Marino: Also Catholic. *Any outreach* by evangelical
believers has resulted in jailing and *expulsion.*

Malta: staunchly Catholic with high church attendance …
Catholic charismatic groups have grown.

Pray that leaders centre their ministry on the Bible

Listen to my cry for help, my King and my God, for to you I pray.
Psalm 5:2

DAY 4

India

○ ○ ○ ○ ○ ○ ○ ○ ○ ○ ○ ○ ○ ○ ○ ○

Praise God for Christianity's two millennia in India

The Holy Spirit has used countless thousands of Indian and expatriate workers to affect India for good in education, health, challenging social wrongs, and to plant over 300,000 churches.

Praise God for continued freedom for Indian Christians to proclaim the gospel!

In him the whole building is joined together and rises to become a holy temple in the Lord. Ephesians 2:21

1 billion people   2.4% Christian

O   O   O   O   O   O   O   O   O   O   O   O   O   O   O

India has more
(and larger) people groups with

no Christians,
churches or workers
than any other part of the world

A rapid increase in intimidation and violence against Muslims
and, in the 1990s, Christians. 70 million child labourers …
10m blind people … half the 1 billion population
functionally illiterate … 600m live in deep poverty

DAY 5

Algeria (Arab world)

O O O O O O O O O O O O O O O

Algeria has long been plagued by clannishness and divisions

Democratic elections in 1992 gave victory to an Islamic political party, but the results were annulled by the army … 100,000 deaths in the ensuing civil war

The Berber peoples may comprise as much as 40% of the population

Thousands have turned to Christ

Pray for strong indigenous Christian groups, protection of Arab believers in persecution, strengthening of Christian families

For you have been my refuge, a strong tower against the foe.
Psalm 61:3

Namibia, Lesotho, Swaziland
(Southern Africa)

O O O O O O O O O O O O O O O

Christian for generations
– some strong evangelical communities
– but traditionalism and nominalism are

widespread

The churches are not holding their young people

These are the AIDS heartlands:
20-25% of the adults here are infected

o o o o o o o o o o o o o o

The largest unreached nation in the world

Few of its 66 million Muslims have ever heard the gospel.
A small Evangelical Church: 2,000 believers in 2000, up from 10 in 1960

Barriers of prejudice

and hatred of the

gospel can seem

insurmountable

Now to him who is able to do immeasurably more than all we ask or imagine. Ephesians 3:20

Endless WARS

Over 2 million deaths through war

genocide and famine since 1983 (Sudan) ... Two decades of unremitting war have brought most of the population to ruin and destitution (Afghanistan) ... Devastated by 30 years of war (Eritrea, East Africa) ...

Continual warfare since 1942 (Myanmar) ...

An international tragedy; in a state of war for six decades (Jammu & Kashmir, India)

He makes wars cease to the ends of the earth; he breaks the bow and shatters the spear, he burns the shields with fire. 'Be still and know that I am God: I will be exalted among the nations.' Psalm 46:9-10

DAY 7

South Korea (East Asia)

Praise God for the unique Korean Church. It was **founded** on sound indigenous principles, **blessed** with a succession of revivals, **refined** by persecution and is now one of the foremost in the world for missions vision … every level of **society has been impacted and growth has been remarkable**

Challenges: spiritual pride, division, authoritarian leadership. The looming crisis of possible economic and political disaster in North Korea will have an enormous impact on the South.

Botswana and Malawi (Africa)

○ ○ ○ ○ ○ ○ ○ ○ ○ ○ ○ ○ ○ ○ ○

Botswana: Christian majority but given over to immorality and drunkenness. Breakdown of family life. The San (Bushmen of the Kalahari Desert) are all resettled in poverty on the fringes of towns and villages, their way of life destroyed. Several thousand may now be Christian.

Malawi: Deep poverty … Continues to be spiritually the

most receptive country
in central Africa

The gospel has penetrated into nearly every section of society.

DAY 8

Be exalted, O God, above the heavens; let your glory be over all the earth. Psalm 57:11

France

○ ○ ○ ○ ○ ○ ○ ○ ○ ○ ○ ○ ○ ○ ○

France remains historically and culturally Catholic, but there has been a massive numerical decline in both Catholic and mainline Protestant churches. Without a dramatic change, Christianity is doomed to insignificance.

Evangelical Christianity has grown …

over 1,000 evangelical churches have been planted

in the past 20 years. Much of that growth has been among Roma (Gypsies) or migrants. To most French people, the evangelical message is still seen as an alien ideology rather than a home-grown faith.

But now in Christ Jesus you who once were far away have been brought near through the blood of Christ. Ephesians 2:13

Georgia (Eurasia)

○ ○ ○ ○ ○ ○ ○ ○ ○ ○ ○ ○ ○ ○

The economy is only very slowly recovering from the USSR's collapse and civil strife. Over the centuries the Georgian Orthodox Church was the one stable factor preserving Georgian culture and nationalism. Since independence, some Orthodox leaders have sought to deny non-Orthodox Christians the opportunity to

build churches and to

evangelize openly

DAY 9

I wait for you, O LORD; you will answer, O LORD my God. Psalm 38:15

Haiti (Caribbean)

O   O   O   O   O   O   O   O   O   O   O   O   O   O   O

The poorest state in the Western hemisphere

A troubled
history of bloodshed and dictatorships

An estimated 75% of Catholics are actively involved in voodoo

Evangelical Christians have increasingly and openly stood
against voodooism

Vision Haiti in 1997, with a widely supported prayer and fasting
movement, has been seen as a turning point

Be on your guard; stand firm in the faith;
be men of courage; be strong. 1 Corinththians 16:13

Madagascar, Mauritius Réunion, Seychelles (Africa)

○ ○ ○ ○ ○ ○ ○ ○ ○ ○ ○ ○ ○ ○ ○

Madagascar: Protestant Church has had a glorious history of faith in persecution. Spiritual deadness now characterizes many

Pray that Bible Schools return to biblical theology

Mauritius: Evangelism a challenge in this multi-ethnic, multi-religious society – 50% Hindu, 33% Christian, 16% Muslim. Nevertheless, large numbers of Hindus are coming to Jesus

Réunion; Seychelles: Mostly Catholic but many are involved in various forms of spiritism

DAY 10

○ ○ ○ ○ ○ ○ ○ ○ ○ ○ ○ ○ ○ ○

The survival and reviving of the Church in China is one of the decisive events of the 20th century.

The growth of the Church

in China since 1977 has

no parallels in history

The 1,266,000 Protestant members and 1.8 million affiliates in 1949 had become 17m members and maybe 26m affiliates in 2000 as well as a much larger uncounted, but estimated, 45m house church Christians. The Catholics grew from 3m to 12m over the same period.

1.2 billion people   7.25% Christian

○ ○ ○ ○ ○ ○ ○ ○ ○ ○ ○ ○ ○ ○ ○

There may only be a ten-year window of opportunity.
Materialism, corruption, moral decline, and the social impact
of the one-child policy all work together to blunt the

cutting edge of the Church

*Pray that the present openness in the midst
of opposition may be used to the full*

DAY 11

He will be the sure foundation for your times, a rich store of
salvation and wisdom and knowledge; the fear of the LORD is
the key to this treasure. Isaiah 33:6

Papua New Guinea (Pacific)

O O O O O O O O O O O O O O O O

About 1,000 peoples, speaking 816 languages.
The government faces a daunting task of uniting such
variety. 80% of the population is still living at subsistence level.

The gospel has spread throughout PNG: 96% claim
to be Christian. Praise God for an alive, vibrant church.

But, for the majority,
it is a superficial Christianity
without a

radical

transformation

of basic values and beliefs

And we, who with unveiled faces all reflect the Lord's glory,
are being transformed into his likeness with ever-increasing glory,
which comes from the Lord, who is the Spirit. 2 Corinthians 3:18

Tunisia (Arab world)

Islamic state but most people

are more committed to **secular**

dreams of wealth

A *concerted prayer movement* in 1999 coincided with

significant numbers

(for such a small church)

of people turning to Christ

DAY 12

Mozambique (Southern Africa)

O O O O O O O O O O O O O O O

Mozambique emerged broken

and wounded from colonialism and three decades of civil war.
In 1995 it was reckoned to be the world's poorest nation

The government has worked hard to open up the economy,
lay true democratic foundations, grant religious freedom, and

bind up the wounds of the past

Intense suffering created spiritual hunger and congregations of
indigenous Christians sprang up all over the country.
Evangelicals: 4% in 1975, 12% in 2000

I will bind up the injured and strengthen the weak. Ezekiel 34:16

Portugal (Europe)

The Roman Catholic Church is strongly traditional
and has much influence, but needs renewal

An estimated 90% of the population consult spiritist
mediums and witches

**25 years of religious freedom
have resulted in the steady
and increased growth of
Evangelicals from 55,000 in
1975 to over 307,000 in 2000**

But let all who take protection in you be glad ... spread your
protection over them. Psalm 5:11

Honduras (Latin America)

O   O   O   O   O   O   O   O   O   O   O   O   O   O   O

Hurricane Mitch in 1998 left millions destitute.

The government is seeking genuine democratic rule,
but is hampered by a culture of crime, institutional
violence and a corrupt judicial system
that protects the privileged.

Evangelicals
growing

for the past 40 years (now 20%)

Arise, LORD! Lift up your hand, O God. Do not forget the helpless.
Psalm 10:12

Gujarat (India)

O O O O O O O O O O O O O O
50 million people   0.5% Christian

Gujarat is a focal point in India for the persecution of Christians … a long-term strategy of intimidation, slander and harassment of Muslims and Christians … 34 churches destroyed or damaged in 1998.

Gujarat was Gandhi's birthplace …
May the peace and tolerance he promoted become reality here.

DAY 14

The Philippines (Southeast Asia)

O O O O O O O O O O O O O O O

**Dramatic growth in the number
of evangelical churches (approaching 40,000 by 2000)**

Manila is a mega-city of enormous challenge

but God is working

Much prayer since 1985 has brought about positive change
Over 15% of the population is linked to an evangelical church

Many Filipinos have gone to difficult and 'closed' countries to be
witnesses for Christ, and some have suffered much for the gospel

*Pray for all Christians that they may
shine for him*

Blind, deaf and disabled people

○ ○ ○ ○ ○ ○ ○ ○ ○ ○ ○ ○ ○ ○ ○

The blind,

deaf and disabled are

often neglected

by society *(Lebanon)*

… 60 million disabled, 13m blind (*China*) … Little has been done to reach the deaf, blind and other handicapped (*Chile*) … 10m blind represent over a quarter of the world's total (*India*) … The elderly and handicapped suffer the most. Health services are grim (*Kyrgyzstan*).

The Spirit of the Lord is on me;
because he has anointed me to preach good news to the poor.
He has sent me to proclaim freedom for the prisoners
and recovery of sight for the blind,
to release the oppressed,
to proclaim the year of the Lord's favour. Luke 4:18-19

DAY 15

Zimbabwe (Southern Africa)

o o o o o o o o o o o o o o

Virtual dictatorship … Zimbabwe needs a government
that will serve the nation rather than those who govern.

AIDS calamity is one of the world's worst:
25% of adults carried the virus in 2000

Strong church growth in the 1980s accelerated in the '90s

The goal of doubling the number of churches from

10,000 in 1992 to 20,000 in 2000 was reached!

Children (Latin America)

○ ○ ○ ○ ○ ○ ○ ○ ○ ○ ○ ○ ○ ○ ○

Over 80% live in extreme poverty (*Bolivia*) …
10 million make their living from the streets
(*Brazil*) …

Over 350,000
children were *abandoned*
during the civil war (*El Salvador*) …

Up to 600,000 sleep rough
(*Mexico*) … Street children have
multiplied in Lima (*Peru*)

Awake, O Lord! Why do you sleep? Rouse yourself!
Psalm 44:23

DAY 16

Sri Lanka (South Asia)

○ ○ ○ ○ ○ ○ ○ ○ ○ ○ ○ ○ ○ ○ ○

Ugly conflict between Sinhala and Tamil peoples has brought great suffering (100,000 killed). The spirit world and idolatry underlie the present evils in Sri Lanka.

Evangelicals have reversed the traditional Christian decline

with a surge of spiritual life

and vigour. The 30,000 villages are a challenge: only 1,200 have Protestant church groups.

Declare his glory among the nations, his marvellous deeds among all peoples. 1 Chronicles 16:24

Libya (Arab world)

O O O O O O O O O O O O O O O

Pray for this tightly-shut land to open to the gospel

A number of expatriate workers are seeking to reach Libyans, but are hindered by the elaborate secret police networks. The Christian community is large, but foreign.

No more than a handful of Libyan believers

DAY 17

My God turns my darkness into light. Psalm 18:28

Bulgaria (Eastern Europe)

O O O O O O O O O O O O O O O

Answers to prayer:

1) Bulgaria's transformation from harsh repression in the 1980s to today's relative freedom of religion and hunger for spirituality

2) The first major breakthrough
for the gospel in modern times in a Turkic people with possibly 10,000 Turkish Millet coming to Christ in the 1990s

Religious freedom is still not fully achieved... Some Orthodox leaders have orchestrated a virulent media campaign against non-Orthodox, and particularly Evangelicals...

Pray for bridges of trust to be built between the major Christian bodies

Zambia (Southern Africa)

○ ○ ○ ○ ○ ○ ○ ○ ○ ○ ○ ○ ○ ○ ○

The Spirit of God has moved through the country with many coming to personal faith in Christ

President Chiluba's government began well in 1991 but has not maintained democratic freedoms nor improved the quality of life for most. Chiluba openly dedicated Zambia to God ... disappointing outworking ... many in the government becoming ostentatiously wealthy

while half the population
live in dire poverty

The AIDS catastrophe has devastated the population

Answer me when I call to you, O my righteous God. Psalm 4:1

Paraguay (Latin America)

○ ○ ○ ○ ○ ○ ○ ○ ○ ○ ○ ○ ○ ○

Still suffers the effects of two centuries of
tyranny, **war** and **government incompetence**

The Roman Catholic Church has long dominated spiritual
and political life … it speaks out against immorality and
corruption, but tolerates much superstitious traditionalism.
Evangelical church growth continued through the 1990s.

Paraguay has never had a true
spiritual awakening

You answer us with awesome deeds of rightousness, O God our
Saviour, the hope of all the ends of the earth and of the farthest
seas. Psalm 65:5

Belarus (Eurasia)

○ ○ ○ ○ ○ ○ ○ ○ ○ ○ ○ ○ ○ ○ ○ ○

The Chernobyl catastrophe in 1986 occurred in the Ukraine, but affected Belarus most severely. Twenty-five percent of the land area is uninhabitable. Radiation-related health problems still occur at 80 times the global average.

Pray that God may use believers as ministers of
restoration and hope

Many call themselves Christian [but] a great need for renewal within the large Orthodox and Catholic structures.

Evangelical Christians are increasing
despite low-level persecution.

DAY 19

Pakistan (South Asia)

O O O O O O O O O O O O O O O

Inept and corrupt civilian and military governments.
An Islamic republic. *Shari'a* law increasingly applied.

Persecution a growing reality since 1991

Everything conspires to make Christians fearful and silent, yet

the Church has grown

Muslim-background Christians particularly under threat; possibly
thousands of secret believers but only a small number identify
openly as Christians

All too often, **believers**
have the double trauma of

rejection

by their community and then

non-acceptance

by the Christian community

156 million people   2% Christian

O   O   O   O   O   O   O   O   O   O   O   O   O   O   O

50% of the population is under 15. Only 25% of children go to school. Child labour exploits between 6 and 20 million

Drug abuse a problem
Youth ministries few and small

Unreached peoples: Over 160 ethnic groups and 40 language groups do not have viable, indigenous congregations or an effective cross-cultural missions initiative.

Few countries present a greater challenge for missions

DAY 20

I spread out my hands to you; my soul thirsts for you like a parched land. Psalm 143:6

Egypt (Arab world)

By far the largest body of Christians in the Middle East

The Church has come through nearly 2,000 years
of discrimination and times of severe persecution, yet has
retained its strong spiritual character

Persecution of Christians steadily increased
in intensity during the 1980s and '90s

*In the last few years over 1,300 Christians
have died at the hands of Islamists*

The LORD will make himself known to the Egyptians, and in that day
they will acknowledge the LORD. Isaiah 19:21

Dominican Republic (Caribbean)

O O O O O O O O O O O O O O O O

Sugar cane has been the source of 500 years of wealth and misery (for example, exploitation of the large Haitian under-class by the rich; now also EU rich-world distortion of the world sugar market through cheap exports)

40% live in deep poverty

Pray for fair treatment of the poor by both the Dominican government and richer nations

Catholicism is the state religion. Evangelical growth came relatively late but during the '90s the number of evangelical churches increased from about 2,000 to 3,200.

DAY 21

Angola (Southern Africa)

○ ○ ○ ○ ○ ○ ○ ○ ○ ○ ○ ○ ○ ○ ○

Continual war since 1962 has been devastating …

100,000 amputees

… The psychological, social and spiritual wounds
are even more harmful and long-lasting

*Pray for the healing of the nation at
every level*

Congregations have multiplied,
services are packed

and despite their desperation
and destitution hundreds
of thousands have trusted
in the Lord Jesus Christ

He heals the brokenhearted and binds up their wounds. Psalm 147:3

Environment

China:

Faces environmental disasters on many fronts: deforestation, the unknown impact of the Three Gorges Dam, polluted rivers, nine of the ten most polluted cities in the world

Madagascar:

Slash-and-burn farming has destroyed vast areas. Eco-tourism has great potential if the country's rich bio-diversity is not destroyed

Maldives:

Global warming threatens the survival of the Islands through rising sea levels

Where were you when I laid the earth's foundation? Tell me, if you understand. Job 38:4

India's unreached peoples

O O O O O O O O O O O O O O O

The Brahmin (40 million) are the highest caste in the Hindu world … maybe only 18,000 openly profess Christianity.

Other Forward Castes - the Rajput (40m), Mahratta (28m), Jat (12m), Bhumihar (4m), Arora (3.8m), and Samon (3.7m) may have no more than 5,000 Christians … little effective ministry among them.

Many Backward Caste peoples - the Yadava (31.5m), Kurmi (25.7m), Ahir (25.4m), Gujar (8.5m), Sonar (7.1m) - have no known Christians, or only a few thousand.

O you who hear prayer, to you all men will come. Psalm 65:2

Mongolia (Asia)

O O O O O O O O O O O O O O O

The daunting economic situation is a major challenge for the government and deeply affects every aspect of life - much unemployment, poverty, 200,000 malnourished children

Probably over half the population practice
Buddhism and/or Shamanism

The Church in **Mongolia**

is a reality for the first time
in modern history

But there are challenges: disunity …
Christianity still too foreign … misconceptions …
many people are 'Christians' only for a year or two …

DAY 23

Be joyful in hope, patient in affliction, faithful in prayer. Romans 12:12

Former Yugoslavia

O O O O O O O O O O O O O O O O

Serbian nationalism, based on centuries of resentment, has wreaked havoc in the Balkans since 1991.
The 'ethnic cleansings' of Catholic Croats, and Bosnian and Albanian Muslims, have left a bitter legacy of

hatred and revenge atrocities

These issues will haunt Europe for decades to come if there are no effective political, economic and, above all, spiritual solutions.

Pray that the tiny evangelical community
might prove a catalyst for good

I lift up my eyes to you, to you whose throne is in heaven. Psalm 123:1

Former Yugoslavia

○ ○ ○ ○ ○ ○ ○ ○ ○ ○ ○ ○ ○ ○ ○

Serbia has one of the lowest percentages of Evangelicals in Europe ... *Montenegro* is nominally Orthodox; very few Evangelicals ... *Kosovar Albanian* population is almost entirely Muslim, but there are some Christians ... *Slovenia* has a strong Catholic tradition. However, the three main Christian groups (Catholic, Orthodox, Lutheran) have little spiritual vitality. *Macedonia's* evangelical witness is small, but growing ... *Croatia*: Evangelical growth during the 1990s among the Croat majority ... *Bosnia*: the minuscule evangelical witness has grown since 1991. Evangelicals

have gained credibility

as the only ones to bridge the gulf between ethnic groups

DAY 24

Israel

O O O O O O O O O O O O O O O

The intense half-century of conflict between
Arabs and Israelis urgently needs resolution

Pray for a just, lasting settlement

The return of Jews to Israel accelerated after the collapse of Communism
Most have returned to their ancient land in unbelief

Pray for the nation's spiritual restoration through Messiah Jesus

Brothers, my heart's desire and prayer to God for the
Israelites is that they may be saved. Romans 10:1

Guyana, Suriname, French Guiana (Latin America/Caribbean)

O   O   O   O   O   O   O   O   O   O   O   O   O   O   O

Guyana; Suriname: Colonial importation of labour has created the present racial diversity: South Asians, East Asians, Africans, Amerindians, Europeans; Christians, Hindus, and Muslims.

Inter-racial tensions ... growing evangelical witness ... Some multi-racial congregations are the only bridge in a divided society

French Guiana: For years infamous as a French penal colony. Now the Kourou satellite launching site is the major source of income. Almost 80% of births are illegitimate, and

indifference to spiritual things is widespread

The LORD is good to those whose hope is in him, to the one who seeks him. Lamentations 3:25

Tanzania (East Africa)

o o o o o o o o o o o o o o

51% Christian, 32% Muslim

Dramatic growth of evangelicals in the 1990s (to 17% in 2000) ...

move of the Holy Spirit in many denominations

Intercommunal balance and political stability cannot be taken for granted. AIDS continues its frightening growth: 8% afflicted

Then the church ... enjoyed a time of peace. It was strengthened; and encouraged by the Holy Spirit, it grew in numbers, living in the fear of the Lord. Acts 9:31

Kyrgyzstan (Central Asia)

O O O O O O O O O O O O O O O

Poorest and smallest of the Central Asian Republics

**The economic situation affects, and depresses, everyone
The elderly and handicapped suffer the most**

**Fear of the 'evil eye', use of amulets, the occult, shaman priests and demonization
are widespread**

Unprecedented opportunity to believe in the Lord Jesus Christ

The Kyrgyz Church has grown from 20 believers in 1990 to over 3,200 in 2000.

Pray that churches become viable and gain permission to register officially

DAY 26

Thailand (Southeast Asia)

O   O   O   O   O   O   O   O   O   O   O   O   O   O   O

A complex web of culture, spirit appeasement,
occult practices, and Buddhism, with a social
cohesiveness out of which few have dared to come.

Corrupt leaders defend the sex trade, the drug networks, the crime syndicates and the environmental degradation

Disappointing church growth. Yet, expectancy.
Christians 0.6% in 1900, 0.9% in 1985, but 1.6% in 2000

Media

○ ○ ○ ○ ○ ○ ○ ○ ○ ○ ○ ○ ○ ○ ○

Scripture translation: 94% of the world's population has access to an understandable New Testament translation (or soon will, through existing translation projects)

Radio: 99% of the world's people potentially can hear Christian radio programming in a language they can understand

The *JESUS* film has been seen by perhaps

3 billion people

As the rain and the snow come down from heaven, and do not return to it without watering the earth and making it bud and flourish ... so is my word that goes out from my mouth: It will not return to me empty. Isaiah 55:10-11

Uganda (East Africa)

O   O   O   O   O   O   O   O   O   O   O   O   O   O

Inter-tribal warfare and government incompetence racked the country. Yoweri Museveni gained power in 1986 and has gradually brought a measure of stability unknown for 25 years

Government and churches faced up to the terrible calamity of AIDS … numbers afflicted reduced from 25% in 1992 to possibly 8-10% in 2000

Widespread prayer movements …

amazing growth

of the Pentecostal Assemblies and a gospel-preaching revival movement in the Catholic Church

El Salvador (Latin America)

○ ○ ○ ○ ○ ○ ○ ○ ○ ○ ○ ○ ○ ○ ○

Recovery – from the wounds of centuries of
oppression and from 12 years of civil war – is a priority

The growth of Evangelicals has been
a modern-day miracle

(22% of the population in 2000)

Pray for effective
discipling

DAY 28

You are the God who performs miracles;
you display your power among the peoples. Psalm 77:14

A continued relative openness to the gospel continues despite, or even because of:
- the increased Islamist propaganda and violence
- disillusionment with politicians
- a series of natural disasters

The churches have been growing at twice the population rate

over the past 40 years. **Still only 0.3%** of the population, Christians are having an increasing impact.

Bangladesh

129 million people   86% Muslim, 12% Hindu

The downward spiral of poverty and suffering cannot be reversed without good, honest and impartial leadership for the nation

The majority of the population is illiterate, malnourished and without adequate medical care

May the poor and needy praise your name. Rise up O God and defend your cause. Psalm 74:21-22

DAY 29

Democratic Republic of Congo
formerly Zaire (Central Africa)

○ ○ ○ ○ ○ ○ ○ ○ ○ ○ ○ ○ ○ ○ ○

Congo's war involved seven nations

Stimulated by the nation's calamities, there has been a large increase, involving millions, **in commitment to prayer**

The result is full churches and a hunger for God

The Christian Church has a crucial role in rebuilding the nation

They all joined together constantly in prayer. Acts 1:14

Xinjiang (China)

O   O   O   O   O   O   O   O   O   O   O   O   O   O   O

Rich natural resources and strategic location.
Uyghur separatism, fuelled by Islamist support from the
Middle East and Central Asia, has increased over the 1990s

vigorous repression ...
thousands executed

There were believers and churches among the Uyghur in the 1930s,
but the churches were destroyed and believers killed or scattered. Only
a few Uyghur believers in Xinjiang now, but nearly 500 in Kazakhstan.
The 360,000 Christians in Xinjiang, almost all Han Chinese,
are culturally isolated from the Uyghur.

DAY 30

Be faithful, even to the point of death, and I will give you the crown
of life. Revelation 2:10

Palestinian Authority

O O O O O O O O O O O O O O O

Two separate parts - the West Bank and the Gaza Strip. The Palestine Authority controls the main towns and scattered enclaves. The rest is made up of 240 Jewish settler enclaves and areas controlled by the Israeli military authorities.

Pray for:

- A fair settlement of the land issue

- The future for Palestinian exiles. (Two million live in 61 refugee camps in surrounding lands)

- Christian Palestinians. Numbers have declined dramatically from around 10% in 1940 to 1.4% in 2000

Why, O LORD, do you stand far off? Psalm 10:1

o o o o o o o o o o o o o o o

80 million people

Christians declined in census statistics from 0.92% in 1981 to 0.64% in 1991, but there is much encouragement at the grass-roots. Christian institutions, especially Catholic ones, have had a positive impact.

DAY 31

His intent was that now, through the church, the manifold wisdom of God should be made known to the rulers and authorities in the heavenly realms, according to his eternal purpose which he accomplished in Christ Jesus our Lord. Ephesians 3:10,11

○ ○ ○ ○ ○ ○ ○ ○ ○ ○ ○ ○ ○ ○ ○ ○ ○

Pray for reconciliation

between Tutsi and Hutu and for peace…

centuries of oppression and killings, pain and hatred

Revival in the 1950s brought blessing and great church growth, but a generation later the land has been devastated. The Church is the only institution where reconciliation could begin.

Thousands of spiritual leaders were murdered – for example, all 60 of Rwanda's IFES Bible study leaders.

Lord intervene and change hearts
Bring revival and healing
Reveal Your forgiving power!

Puerto Rico (Caribbean)

○ ○ ○ ○ ○ ○ ○ ○ ○ ○ ○ ○ ○ ○ ○

Traditionally Catholic,
but Evangelicals have grown rapidly to nearly 30% in 2000

AIDS, alcoholism, drug addiction, corruption, crime and poverty

are some of the highest in the Americas

So then, just as you received Christ Jesus as Lord, continue to live in him. Colossians 2:6

Indonesia (Southeast Asia)

○ ○ ○ ○ ○ ○ ○ ○ ○ ○ ○ ○ ○ ○ ○

4,000 inhabited islands; 213 million people – the world's fourth most populous country. Years of economic improvement came to a stunning halt in 1997. Government

faces a daunting task

All citizens must choose one of five religions: Islam, Hinduism, Buddhism or Christianity (Protestant or Catholic). Creeping Islamization

Therefore in the east give glory to the LORD; exalt the name of the LORD, the God of Israel, in the islands of the sea. Isaiah 24:15

Indonesia

Some islands of Indonesia: *Sumatra* is the largest unevangelised island on earth with 52 unreached people groups consisting of 25 million people

Java: As never before, traditional Protestant, Evangelical and Pentecostal churches have united in prayer. A spiritual, moral and missions awakening … cell church movement is

rapidly expanding… a time of harvest!

Maluku: A tragic cycle of revenge led to both Muslim and some Christian atrocities. Enormous destruction of property … over 400 churches and some mosques

Pray for an end to the conflict, communal harmony restored and the deep wounds healed

DAY 33

Ukraine (Eurasia)

o o o o o o o o o o o o o o

The nation is beginning to climb out of its post-Communist economic disaster. The vacuum left by Communism has often been filled with violent crime, breakdown in family structures and sexual immorality. Radiation pollution from Chernobyl still affects huge swathes of the country

Much superstition and superficiality

in the Orthodox and Catholic churches, but also a spiritual minority with a love for the Scriptures. Since independence, evangelical churches have nearly doubled

Further growth could be hampered by
lack of resources

Night and day we pray most earnestly ... 1 Thessalonians 3:10

Switzerland (Europe)

○　○　○　○　○　○　○　○　○　○　○　○　○　○　○

The falling away of the Swiss from both Catholic and
Reformed churches is gaining momentum

This is only partially offset by the growth of Pentecostal,
charismatic and evangelical free churches

A strong, growing prayer movement
is raising expectancy for revival

DAY 34

Argentina (Latin America)

O O O O O O O O O O O O O O O

Renewal,
much prayer and
large-scale evangelism

since 1983 have deeply affected the nation and touched the world through Argentinean evangelists, teachers, missionaries and leaders

Prison ministry has revolutionized the nation's jails

Landmines

- over 12 million uncleared anti-personnel mines **Afghanistan**

- outnumber the population **Angola**

- over 30,000 have lost limbs to them **Cambodia**

How long, O LORD? Psalm 79:5

Timor Lorosae ('East Timor', Southeast Asia)

○ ○ ○ ○ ○ ○ ○ ○ ○ ○ ○ ○ ○ ○ ○ ○

Independent of Indonesia in 1999. Traumatic birth

Militia supported by the Indonesian army looted and destroyed the new country before the UN stepped in

Catholic Church grew fast as a visible symbol of national resistance, but the **deep occultism** of the ethnic religions

remains strong

Pray that evangelical churches may be planted in every people and area

Kerala (India)

○ ○ ○ ○ ○ ○ ○ ○ ○ ○ ○ ○ ○ ○

33 million people   19% Christian

The Syrian Christians – descendants of those evangelized by the Apostle Thomas – form the majority of Kerala's Christians and are members of Orthodox, Catholic and Protestant denominations

A revived Church

in Kerala would have a
**deep impact
on all of India…**
a surge of interest in
missions since the
mid-1990s

The Lord gives strength to his people; the Lord blesses his people with peace. Psalm 29:11

UK & Ireland

o o o o o o o o o o o o o o o

UK: Spiritual need is highlighted by increasing violence in the cities, the high divorce, suicide and illegitimacy rates, and drug abuse ... a growing number of younger people have no contact with Christianity

Pray for national repentance and restoration

Evangelical Christians are basically maintaining numbers, despite considerable church decline

Ireland (Eire): Involvement in the Catholic Church declining quite fast. Hundreds of evangelical fellowships multiplying and growing across the Republic

Pray that the wounds in Irish society might be healed and the whole of Ireland be at peace

Seek the LORD while he may be found; call on him while he is near.
Isaiah 55:6

The Fulbe ('Fulani', 'Fula', 'Peul') (West Africa)

O O O O O O O O O O O O O O

A 20-million-strong Muslim people

Twelve million live in Nigeria. Some form the ruling class there. Others are nomadic cattle grazers across Nigeria and the Sahel

*Pray that God may
give the right strategies for reaching both
groups – the nomadic cattle people being a
particular challenge*

If the gospel gripped this group,
all West Africa would be affected!

He provided redemption for his people; he ordained his covenant
forever— holy and awesome is his name. Psalm 111:9

China's Communists

O O O O O O O O O O O O O O O

China has nearly 60 million Communist Party members

Among them are many secret believers

Disillusionment

and defection to Christianity has led to many resignations

Pray that the Holy Spirit will convict many more of their sin and need

In your majesty ride forth victoriously on behalf of truth, humility
and righteousness; let your right hand display awesome deeds.
Psalm 45:4

Kenya (East Africa)

O O O O O O O O O O O O O O O

13 million Evangelicals –
nearly equal to all Evangelicals in Europe

Pray that Christians
> *may bring truth*
>> *and moral uplift*

… the nation edges to the brink of political disaster with
possible economic collapse and inter-ethnic conflict

Nominalism is a major issue. The capital Nairobi is 80%
'Christian', but only 12% of the population goes to church

DAY 38

o o o o o o o o o o o o o o o

Freedom
of religion

Eighteen recognized religious communities: four Muslim,
Druze, Jewish and 12 Christian

A number from the Hizbollah
faction and several hundred
Druze have come to Christ

There are Christians among the
Palestinians, some evangelical, but the majority are
Muslim and unreached

Expatriate Christian workers
are returning to Lebanon after years away

Panama (Latin America)

○ ○ ○ ○ ○ ○ ○ ○ ○ ○ ○ ○ ○ ○ ○

Rapid recovery from the desperate days of Noriega's misrule...

new hope
for the future

Continued spiritual responsiveness

Evangelicals have grown from 4.8% of the population in 1970 to 18% in 2000

A prayer movement among pastors is

s p r e a d i n g

DAY 39

Never be lacking in zeal, but keep your spiritual fervor, serving the Lord. Romans 12:11

Bihar and Jharkhand (India)

O O O O O O O O O O O O O

103 million people   1-2% Christian

North Bihar is one of the least evangelized mega-populations in the world. It has long been known as a graveyard of missions. Years of effort have yielded little fruit among the Hindu and Muslim people of the plains. **Christian churches are in great need**

Bihar has become a byword for corruption, Mafia-style politics, a breakdown of law and order, communal tensions oppression of minorities and underdevelopment

I am the vine; you are the branches. John 15:5

Jordan (Arab world)

O O O O O O O O O O O O O O O

Little access to the gospel for the Muslim majority,
the millions of Palestinians,
      the Iraqi refugees,
            or the 200,000 Bedouin

  This nation is a centre for many Christian ministries

*Pray for peace, the King and the government,
and preservation of religious freedom*

Jordan's Christian population (mostly Orthodox and
Catholic) halved between 1970 and 2000. Evangelical
churches, though, are growing

DAY 40

Somalia (East Africa)

○ ○ ○ ○ ○ ○ ○ ○ ○ ○ ○ ○ ○ ○ ○

Economy in ruins, controlled by warlords
Population dependent on food aid

The most lawless country in the world

Christians have fled, been driven underground, or martyred

Globally there may be 2,000 Somali Christians

Their sins and lawless acts I will remember no more. Hebrews 10:17

o o o o o o o o o o o o o o o o

Praise God

for political survival and economic growth despite Mainland China's threats and propaganda

Christian growth, though slow,
resumed in the 1990s after 30 years of stagnation

Taiwan remains the only major Han Chinese
population in the world where the
spiritual breakthrough has yet to come

DAY 41

I wait for the LORD; my soul waits, and in his word I put my hope.
Psalm 130:5

Jakarta and Surabaya (Indonesia)

○ ○ ○ ○ ○ ○ ○ ○ ○ ○ ○ ○ ○ ○ ○

Jakarta and Surabaya are key cities for the gospel in Indonesia. **Almost every ethnic group has a presence there**

Jakarta (the capital) is now over 13% Christian, with over **1,000 registered churches and thousands of cell groups**

A spiritual movement

in Jakarta and Surabaya is having an impact on the whole country

I have many people in this city. Acts 18:10

Moldova (Eastern Europe)

O O O O O O O O O O O O O O O

One of Europe's poorest countries

80% of men are unemployed, 60% have a serious alcohol problem

The Orthodox Church has regained strong political influence
and is not afraid to use it against those it sees as a threat

*Pray that the Holy Spirit would deepen the
spiritual life of many in Moldova from the
Orthodox faith*

Protestant churches are

multiplying

Moldovan-flavoured renewal is occurring, especially among the Gagauz Turks

DAY 42

Italy

This **great and gifted** nation has decisively affected the world, yet is in deep spiritual need. Most Italians are Catholic in culture, but deeply cynical about the Church

Occultism is widespread

Satanism is strong in the north

The Protestant witness is weak and divided

The need for expatriate missionaries is great but the casualty rate has been high, with only 10% returning for a second term

Send forth your light and your truth. Psalm 43:3

Nicaragua (Latin America)

○ ○ ○ ○ ○ ○ ○ ○ ○ ○ ○ ○ ○ ○ ○

**Two centuries of dictatorships,
civil wars and natural calamities**

Nine thousand people killed and two million
made homeless by Hurricane Mitch in 1998.
It may take fifteen years to repair the damage.
International aid quickly dried up

A remarkable turning to God

Evangelicals were 2% of the population in 1960, 20% in 2000

DAY 43

Ethiopia (East Africa)

Praise God for the thrilling growth of the Protestant churches since 1936 … great seasons of harvest with

millions coming to Christ

The Ethiopian Orthodox Church is going through immense change

Pray for a deep work of the Holy Spirit to bring this ancient Church to its biblical heritage and to new life

Hostilities with Eritrea have crippled efforts to revive and modernize the country … Ethnic fragmentation remains a real possibility

Peacemakers who sow in peace raise a harvest of righteousness.
James 3:18

Karachi (Pakistan)

o o o o o o o o o o o o o o o

Maybe 16 million people
A lawless city

inter-ethnic conflicts, an estimated
one million drug addicts,
kidnappings and violent crime
Yet, a key to reaching
Pakistan with the gospel

*Pray for outreach and church-planting
teams for every ethnic group in the city*
especially for the Urdu-speaking Mohajirs, the 500,000
Ismaili Muslims, the 7,000 wealthy Parsees and numerous
Afghan refugees

DAY 44

Awake, my God; decree justice. Psalm 7:6

North Korea (East Asia)

○ ○ ○ ○ ○ ○ ○ ○ ○ ○ ○ ○ ○ ○ ○ ○

One of the most repressive regimes in the world
All religions have been harshly repressed

Little is known about today's underground church, only that it has survived amidst great suffering

As many as 3 million died of starvation between 1994 and 2000, yet the government stockpiles rations for the military and refuses assistance on any but the strictest of terms

O LORD, you have seen this; be not silent. Psalm 35:22

Sex industry

An estimated 250,000 *Nepali girls* (mainly in Mumbai) where they are terribly abused; 60-70% are HIV+ and few will reach 25 years *(India)*… Over 60,000 children and 500,000 women are involved. Many more are victims of trafficking to other countries *(Philippines)*… An infamous child-porn and paedophile industry; over 30,000 children enmeshed *(Sri Lanka)*… 20% of all girls between 11 and 17 involved *(Thailand)*… Significant evil trade: children 'exported' to other lands *(Togo, W Africa)*.

DAY 45

Arise, cry out in the night … pour out your heart like water in the presence of the Lord. Lift up your hands to him for the lives of your children. Lamentations 2:19

Denmark, Iceland, Finland

90% Lutheran, *Denmark* needs a fresh visitation from God

Finland: Pray that deep and lasting revival might come to the entire Lutheran church
The Free Churches, both Pentecostal and non-Pentecostal, are relatively small but spiritually vigorous and growing

Iceland: The majority of Icelanders are only nominally Christian. A few pastors and congregations

remain faithful

This calls for patient endurance on the part of the saints who obey God's commandments and remain faithful to Jesus. Revelation 14:12

Norway, Sweden (Europe)

○ ○ ○ ○ ○ ○ ○ ○ ○ ○ ○ ○ ○ ○ ○ ○ ○

Norway: The Lutheran Church is unique in Europe: although it is the State Church, many of the pastors are theologically evangelical … influence of Pietism, prayer and

revival movements still strong

Norway's large contribution to world evangelization continues

Sweden: Nineteenth century was notable for revivals, a vigorous Free Church movement and great commitment to missions. The 20th century was the opposite: rapid secularization and emergence of one of the most permissive societies of Europe

Syria (Arab world)

o o o o o o o o o o o o o o o

Secular state, a measure of religious freedom, but all activities that could threaten the government or communal harmony are watched

Syrian Christians, a respected minority since Acts 13, are influential but are emigrating ...

An evangelical presence in most cities, but rarely in smaller towns
Conversions out of Islam are few, but increasing

The name of the Lord is a strong tower; the righteous run to it and are safe. Proverbs 18:10,11

Beijing (China)

○ ○ ○ ○ ○ ○ ○ ○ ○ ○ ○ ○ ○ ○ ○ ○

China is ruled from Beijing

Pray for the leaders of the nation
- for wisdom,
humanity,
seeking of the good of the people,
and courage to make the long-delayed economic and
political decisions essential for the future

DAY 47

Laos (Southeast Asia)

○ ○ ○ ○ ○ ○ ○ ○ ○ ○ ○ ○ ○ ○ ○ ○

The Church has suffered much since the Communists took over in 1975 and declared it the Number One enemy of the state

Yet it still grows and spreads

Pray for perseverance and grace for those suffering, for leaders for the churches, for Bible translation and literature distribution

Christianity has not moved easily across the diverse ethno-linguistic boundaries, leaving many groups completely unreached

The word of the LORD spread through the whole region. Acts 13:49

Djibouti (East Africa)

O O O O O O O O O O O O O O O

93% Muslim, mostly Afar and Somali peoples
A haven of calm in a stormy region

Mission work is a tough challenge
in this hot, dry but often humid land, and working
conditions are extreme

Pray for ministries in education, public health,
literature, Bible translation, literacy and
youth work

The few Somali and Afar believers are often isolated
and suffer many pressures from relatives. Most of
them are jobless and some are illiterate

I want to know Christ and the power of his resurrection and the
fellowship of sharing in his sufferings, becoming like him in his
death. Philippians 3:10

DAY 48

Canada

O O O O O O O O O O O O O O O O

The Christian Church
has become **marginalized**

Evangelicals as a percentage of population: 25% in 1900;
8% in 1989; 10.8% in 2000

Immigrant communities have multiplied: Asian Indians,
Arabic-speakers, Southern and Eastern Europeans and
Chinese

*Pray for a moving of God's Spirit to overcome the past
shameful treatment of indigenous peoples by whites*

Andhra Pradesh and Karnataka
(India)

O O O O O O O O O O O O O O

Andhra Pradesh (80 million people, 1.9% Christian):

Christian outreach continues

with numerous people coming to Christ. The state capital Hyderabad is the key centre for Islam in South India

Karnataka (54m people, 2.1% Christian): The Christian communities are inward-looking and culturally isolated

Bangalore in Karnataka is India's 'Silicon City' and is also the Indian headquarters for many Christian churches

Pray that Bangalore's privileged Christian community may be revived

DAY 49

The LORD is my stength and my song. Exodus 15:2

Iraq (Arab world)

Twenty years of war, diplomatic isolation and economic disasters have lessened prejudice to the gospel among Muslims and brought an openness to reading the Scriptures

The Christian community has suffered even more than the general population

In its pain nearly every denomination has experienced

some renewal, revival and hunger for God's Word

As for God, his way is perfect; the word of the Lord is flawless. He is a shield for all who take refuge in him. Psalm 18:30

Small Caribbean Countries

Most claim to be Christian … many evangelical … much nominalism … many births out of wedlock Inter-church rivalry has harmed overall witness

Jamaica has sunk into a morass of social and economic problems … Half the male population are drug-abusers …

The spiritual temperature
of Jamaica affects the whole Caribbean

Trinidad's South Asian community is the largest non-Christian community in the Caribbean. Many Hindus and some Muslims have turned to Christ

DAY 50

Eritrea (East Africa)

O O O O O O O O O O O O O O O

48% Muslim   47% Christian

Peace and national recovery have been delayed by conflicts with Ethiopia and Yemen. The Ethiopian war caused the death of 70,000+ Eritreans and Ethiopians in fierce trench warfare.

Freedom of religion is a major issue. Fear of Islamist extremism and Christian evangelicalism has **restricted the entry** of expatriate Christian workers.

I consider that our present sufferings are not worth comparing with the glory that will be revealed in us. Romans 8:18

Hong Kong and Macau (China)

○ ○ ○ ○ ○ ○ ○ ○ ○ ○ ○ ○ ○ ○ ○

Hong Kong: A vital centre for media. Literature is written, printed, published and distributed on a massive scale. Bibles are printed for the world. Studios prepare radio programmes.

Pray that this role may be maintained in the 21st century

Some churches continue to grow vigorously, particularly cell churches. Conversions have replaced losses through emigration.

Macau: The Catholic Church has suffered disastrous decline, and Protestant churches have always been small

DAY 51

Uzbekistan (Central Asia)

○ ○ ○ ○ ○ ○ ○ ○ ○ ○ ○ ○ ○ ○ ○

The people are disillusioned –

crumbling economy, government corruption

Praise God for Uzbek believers

now numbering 1,000+

But much prayer is still needed

Uzbekistan is one of the world's worst violators of religious liberty

Dynamic and evangelism-oriented churches are particularly targeted

'Now, Lord, consider their threats and enable your servants to speak your word with great boldness.' Acts 4:29

The Pope

The Pope is head of
the largest religious
body on earth,
1.1 billion
Catholics

He exercises an

enormous

influence

within and beyond the
Roman Catholic Church

DAY 52

Bhutan (South Asia)

O O O O O O O O O O O O O O O

Strongly isolationist
government that

reinforces the hold of

Tantric Buddhism along with much that is demonic
and occult

The Drukpa majority is strongly Buddhist, and Christians
among them number only a few hundred

The Nepali minority has responded to the gospel and since 1970 there has
been steady growth. 'Ethnic cleansing' of this minority since 1990

Pray for a wise, enlightened government

I guide you in the way of wisdom and lead you along straight paths.
Proverbs 4:11

Greece

○ ○ ○ ○ ○ ○ ○ ○ ○ ○ ○ ○ ○ ○ ○

Christianity is now more cultural than spiritual. Only 2% of the population in church on an average Sunday … A godly minority with a personal faith …

Pray for biblical renewal within Orthodoxy

All other expressions of Christianity are

seen as a threat to the state and the culture

Evangelical church members number only around 15,000

Pray for cultural and legal equality for the non-Orthodox that is consistent with Greece's membership of the EU

DAY 53

Sudan (Arab world/East Africa)

O O O O O O O O O O O O O O O

Bitter fighting between Arab northerners and non-Arab southerners ... declared an Islamic republic in 1983 ... crude attempts to Islamize non-Muslims ... re-institution of slavery ... bombing of church services ... education and health services have barely functioned for two decades.

Christians have spread

all around the country. Massive growth among the Southern peoples. A small but increasing number – some thousands – from the Muslim majority have also become Christians.

But the word of God continued to increase and spread. Acts 12:24

Costa Rica (Latin America)

○ ○ ○ ○ ○ ○ ○ ○ ○ ○ ○ ○ ○ ○ ○ ○

Between 1970 and 1988, dramatic growth of
Evangelicals from 3% to 11%. After problems, growth
has resumed: some reckon 16% to be Evangelicals now

The problems that halted growth:
division, legalism, materialism, moral failure

The Roman Catholic Church has been deeply impacted by
charismatic renewal. Many have come to a living, personal

faith in Christ

DAY 54

I pray that out of his glorious riches he may strengthen you with
power through his Spirit in your inner being. Ephesians 3:16

China's social and health needs

○ ○ ○ ○ ○ ○ ○ ○ ○ ○ ○ ○ ○ ○ ○ ○

China's social and health needs
overwhelm
available resources:

1.9 million with **tuberculosis**, over 300,000 with **HIV/AIDS**,
10m **mentally retarded** through iodine-deficiency, 60m
disabled, 13m **blind** and 520,000 registered **drug addicts**

*Pray that Christians may
find many openings
to show and speak about
the love of Jesus*

Central African Republic

o o o o o o o o o o o o o o o o

Widespread
evangelism

since the 1960s has yielded a massive response. The CAR has Africa's highest percentage of Evangelicals (35%)

But, lack of effective discipleship ...
nominalism ... divisions ... religious pride

And I pray that you, being rooted and established in love, may have power, together with all the saints, to grasp how wide and long and high and deep is the love of Christ and to know this love that surpasses knowledge – that you may be filled to the measure of all the fulness of God. Ephesians 3:18,19

Japan (East Asia)

o o o o o o o o o o o o o o o

Japan is a mixture of **openness** and **unresponsiveness**

The powers associated with idolatry in temples and ancestor worship in homes have never been decisively challenged … Resurgence of a nationalistic Shintoism … An average of 100

new occult religions

are started each year

The ruling elite have been little influenced by the gospel

But for you who revere my name, the sun of righteousness will rise with healing in its wings. Malachi 4:2

The decisive breakthrough

has yet to come for the Church

Denominational fragmentation, theological divides and lack of nation-wide co-operation have hampered progress

Quasi-Christian groups such as the Moonies, Jehovah's Witnesses and Mormons have grown far faster than Evangelicals or Catholics

DAY 56

Poland (Eastern Europe)

O   O   O   O   O   O   O   O   O   O   O   O   O   O   O

The Catholic Church was long the custodian of Polish culture
Its popularity drops with every flex of its political muscles,
accused of trying to create a repressive religious state.

In the 1980s many Catholics came to

personal faith in Christ

as a result of Bible study groups

*Pray that biblical teachings and values
might be retained and enhanced*

Evangelical Christians are a very small minority

Teach me to do your will, for you are my God; may your good Spirit
lead me on level ground. Psalm 143:10

Uruguay (Latin America)

○ ○ ○ ○ ○ ○ ○ ○ ○ ○ ○ ○ ○ ○ ○

Characterized by secularism for over 100 years

Lack of knowledge of God

has given opening to a spirit of error. Brazilian spiritists, once banned, could possibly number a million, many of them members of the Catholic Church. The largest non-Catholic religious bodies are sects such as the Mormons, Jehovah's Witnesses and the New Apostolic Church.

Evangelical churches have struggled to make an impact. However, since 1986 the growth of some Pentecostal groups and Baptists has

accelerated

DAY 57

West Bengal (India)

82 million people
480,000 'Christians' of whom
probably 95% are nominal

The state capital Kolkata
(Calcutta) is dedicated to Kali,
the Hindu goddess of
destruction

It has the lowest urban standard of living in the world …
vast slums … a million or more living on the streets

I have come that they may have life, and have it to the full.
John 10:10

Congo & Gabon (West Africa)

O O O O O O O O O O O O O O O

The majority in each country were baptized Catholic,
but a large number still follow the old animist ways.

Congo: revival and restoration is the Church's need after two decades of Communist dictatorship followed by civil war.

Gabon: conversion of the President to Islam … secret societies … alcoholism… widespread ignorance of the gospel. But the 1990s have been a time of God's moving in Gabon.

The Church has grown rapidly

And having disarmed the powers and authorities, he made a public spectacle of them, triumphing over them by the cross.
Colossians 2:15

Singapore (Southeast Asia)

O O O O O O O O O O O O O O O

High growth of the Church peaked in the 1980s and
1990s.
It has since slowed and young people are becoming less
responsive

A key Christian base and mission sending country

Christians need sensitivity in a multi-faith context, but
also boldness when fundamental issues of freedom of
religion are challenged

This is the victory that has overcome the world, even our faith.
1 John 5:4

Kuwait (Arab world)

o   o   o   o   o   o   o   o   o   o   o   o   o   o

Since the Iraqi occupation, Kuwait has returned to stability and affluence …

Materialism is rampant
and public morals declining,
but restrictions on Christianity remain

Only a few hundred Kuwaitis are known to be believers

From the ends of the earth I call to you, I call as my heart grows faint; lead me to the rock that is higher than I. Psalm 61:2

Brazil (Latin America)

Continued spiritual hunger has caused many to seek after God. Evangelicals continue to grow in numbers and influence

Spiritism is a dynamic force for evil,
and a majority of Brazilians are involved

Favelas: These slums are a highly visible blight in every major city. Home to nearly 20 million poverty-stricken and needy people, hotbeds of crime, drugs, violence, prostitution and disease, they are rarely entered by the police.

The sacrifices of God are a broken spirit; a broken and contrite heart, O God, you will not despise. Psalm 51:17

Media

India: By 2000, one mission, EHC, had distributed 500 million pieces of literature. They had seen 6m responses and 16,000 Christ Group fellowships formed

Egypt and Arab world: The innovative use of media through literature (*Magalla* magazine) and television (*SAT-7*) has

multiplied the effectiveness of proclaiming the gospel

In countries like *China* and *Vietnam*, large networks of house churches have sprung up through the ministry of Christian radio

Small Pacific Islands

A large proportion of the population is Christian, but nominalism is widespread

Pray for revival

Mormonism and other cults are growing. Some Pentecostal, evangelical, and charismatic growth too

The Indians of *Fiji* form the largest non-Christian community in the Pacific. Only 6% of them claim to be Christian

In his law the islands will put their hope. Isaiah 42:4

China's families

o o o o o o o o o o o o o o o

'One child' policy has deeply impacted family life ...
● a higher *divorce* rate
● ten million *abortions* a year (nearly all girls)
● *suicide* (40% of the world's suicides
are in China)

... in some areas young men outnumber young women by 30-40%

Pray for family stability and health
Pray also for wise policies to be
implemented

DAY 61

God sets the lonely in families. Psalm 68:6

Chad (Central Africa)

O O O O O O O O O O O O O O O

One of the poorest countries in the world

Freedom of religion is a precious reality, but is threatened. The population is almost equally divided between the politically dominant Muslim northerners and the increasingly marginalized Christian/ethnic-religion southerners. Their cultures are so different and their history is one of northerners enslaving southerners.

The annual Chad for Christ campaigns have been used of God

The vision is to reach every village in the country

We continually remember before our God and Father your work produced by faith, your labour prompted by love, and your endurance inspired by hope in our Lord Jesus Christ.
1 Thessalonians 1:3

Cyprus (Southern Europe)

O   O   O   O   O   O   O   O   O   O   O   O   O   O   O

Divided as a result of the Turkish invasion of 1974

The South: The Orthodox Church has long been a refuge and guarantor of Greek Cypriot survival. Church attendance is high at 48%

> *Pray for Holy Spirit renewal movements to bring many to a warm personal faith in Christ*

Evangelical churches among Greeks are few

The North: Almost the entire population is Muslim, but also very secularized. About 10% are regular mosque-goers

DAY 62

How priceless is your unfailing love! Both high and low among men find refuge in the shadow of your wings. Psalm 36:7

Vietnam (Southeast Asia)

O O O O O O O O O O O O O O O O

Communist party still controls all government policy and activity

The country is gradually opening up

A growing, witnessing Church is emerging from years of persecution. Vietnam remains one of the worst persecutors of Christians

A large-scale and sustained turning to God is taking place, in both registered and unregistered churches

Here I am! I stand at the door and knock. If anyone hears my voice and opens the door, I will come in and eat with him, and he with me. Revelation 3:20

Environment

Myanmar: Plundered and impoverished by its own leaders. Teak forests stripped

Russia: Many thousands of square kilometres have been made uninhabitable by nuclear disasters, weapons testing, and the oil industry

Tuvalu: may be the first nation to disappear as a result of global warming

Uzbekistan: Ecological disasters … lack of water … over-irrigation … poor soil … rapid disappearance of the Aral Sea

Pray that impending crises may cause many to find God

O O O O O O O O O O O O O O O

Answers to prayer:

- Stable, democratic government
- Steady growth of Evangelicals (to 16% of the population)

Evangelicals are poised to exercise a pivotal role in the new millennium. The danger remains that goodwill and respect may be eroded by squandered opportunities

Pray against disunity, traditionalism, poor teaching

The middle and upper classes have been far less impacted by the gospel

God answered prayer on behalf of the land. 2 Samuel 21:14

Qinghai Province (China)

○ ○ ○ ○ ○ ○ ○ ○ ○ ○ ○ ○ ○ ○ ○ ○

Huge, high alpine desert province on the Tibetan Plateau

This desolate region is dotted with labour camps. Many

thousands of prisoners

including Christians, have endured great hardship here

*Pray for all prisoners of conscience that their faith
in God might grow and bless those around them*

DAY 64

But join with me in suffering for the gospel, by the power of God.
2 Timothy 1:8

Cameroon (Central Africa)

O O O O O O O O O O O O O O O

Africa's most complex country:
280 languages; 500 or more ethnic groups

The spiritual poverty of the churches is the country's

greatest tragedy:

tribalism, pagan practices, alcoholism and low moral standards. Most in these churches have no concern for the unreached of the north, nor do they have a prophetic voice to address the major ills of society

Pray for deep repentance, lasting deliverance and true revival to take place in Cameroon

Bahrain (Arab world)

○ ○ ○ ○ ○ ○ ○ ○ ○ ○ ○ ○ ○ ○ ○

A political and spiritual key for the whole Gulf area

- Islam impacts life less comprehensively than in surrounding states

- Has provided a good base for Christian ministry for over a century

I call to you, O LORD, every day; I spread out my hands to you.
Psalm 58:9

DAY 65

Malaysia (Southeast Asia)

O O O O O O O O O O O O O O O

Islamization has brought concern to those of other faiths who are nearly half the population

Pray that Christians may not be intimidated by threats, but rather be bold to stand for their constitutional rights and for their heavenly right to proclaim the gospel

. . . **Your labour in the Lord is not in vain.** 1 Corinthians 15:58

Bible Translation

... An enormous unfinished task **(Indonesia)** ...

At the present rate it will take 100 years **(India)** ...

No Scriptures in Libyan Arabic. Pray that work on this may start **(Libya)** ... Maybe up to 55 languages require NT translation teams **(Pakistan)** ...

Translation teams are definitely needed for 135 languages and possibly for a further 466 **(Papua New Guinea)** ... 30m people speak languages that don't have a NT **(Russia)** ... It had been assumed that widespread use of Swahili would have diminished the need.

Yet 45 languages definitely need translation teams **(Tanzania)**

Each one heard them speaking in his own language.
Acts 2:6

Hungary (Eastern Europe)

O O O O O O O O O O O O O O

Peaceful transition from Communist dictatorship to parliamentary democracy

1990s growth: strong charismatic and renewal movements in the Catholic, Baptist, Reformed and other denominations, but not on a scale for which Christians had hoped

Pray for reconciliation of the nation to God, spiritual renewal, restoration and revival

Great need for evangelists

Maharashtra (India)

○ ○ ○ ○ ○ ○ ○ ○ ○ ○ ○ ○ ○ ○ ○
95 million people   1.2% Christian

The state capital Mumbai (formerly Bombay) is home to
India's stock exchange and film industry ('Bollywood')

Also has Asia's **largest slum,** 100,000
street children, child prostitution, and an
alarming rise in AIDS (200,000 sufferers in 1996)

It has many Catholics and a growing number of Protestants

Pray that Christians be 'salt and light' in their city

DAY 67

'You are the light of the world. A city on a hill cannot be hidden.'
Matthew 5:14

Kazakhstan (Central Asia)

O O O O O O O O O O O O O O O

Kazakhs have been nominally Sunni Muslims since 1043,
but theirs is a folk Islam strongly influenced by animistic practices

The Church among Kazakhs is young, but alive and

g r o w i n g strong

Many humanitarian and holistic mission opportunities in
this troubled land

*Pray that the good co-operation between
those ministering here via the 'Kazakh
Partnership' may continue to deepen*

Your arm is endued with power; your hand is
strong, your right hand exalted. Psalm 89:13

Ecuador (Latin America)

○ ○ ○ ○ ○ ○ ○ ○ ○ ○ ○ ○ ○ ○ ○

Political uncertainty, war and a series of natural and economic disasters over the past 20 years have broken down old feudal structures of State and Church and made Ecuadorians more receptive to the gospel

Evangelicals have increased from 0.43% (19,000 people) in 1960 to 6.1% (776,000) in 2000. This growth has been largely in the cities and among the Quichua (Amerindians)

Pray for unity

DAY 68

How good and pleasant it is when brothers live together in unity!
Psalm 133:1

Nigeria (West Africa)

○ ○ ○ ○ ○ ○ ○ ○ ○ ○ ○ ○ ○ ○

Wide differences between feudal, Muslim north and entrepreneurial, largely Christian south … tension, violence, coups and civil war … 111 million population

Culture of greed and corruption … wealth stolen by former leaders is about equal to the national debt of $30 billion

Elections in 1999 brought Olusegun Obasanjo, a committed Christian, to the Presidency. He has wisely and tactfully moved to bring about change.

Spectacular Church growth …
spirit of prayer among Christians

Renewal (Orthodox Church)

O O O O O O O O O O O O O O O

The rapid spread of Scriptures has led to strong evangelical and charismatic networks *(Ethiopia)* … Biblically-based renewal has steadily gained momentum since 1930 *(Egypt)* … In the midst of traditionalism and deadness are also sig nificant renewal movements *(Lebanon)* … The Lord's Army is a remarkable, unofficial renewal movement with 300,000 adherents and many more sympathizers *(Romania)* … The reformers are often persecuted but are more Bible-focused, open for change and tolerant than the traditionalists *(Russia)*

DAY 69

'Not by might, nor by power, but by my Spirit,' says the LORD Almighty. Zechariah 4:6

Nepal (South Asia)

○ ○ ○ ○ ○ ○ ○ ○ ○ ○ ○ ○ ○ ○ ○

Needs political stability after the first tempestuous decade of democracy, and after the traumatic murders in the royal family in 2001. National religion: Hinduism. Some religious freedom

Only 15% of the population have access to electricity
Much is done in education, job creation, water purification, and medical work, by Christians

The Church has flourished

in the midst of pressure as a remarkable indigenous movement
No Christian was officially allowed to live in Nepal before 1960.
By 2000 there were 400,000 - 500,000 Christians

But I trust in your unfailing love. Psalm 13:5

Unreached peoples in Indonesia

O   O   O   O   O   O   O   O   O   O   O   O   O   O   O

The 35 million *Sunda* live in West Java. Christian Sunda number about 12,000 but some are nominal and culturally isolated from the Muslim majority

The Minangkabau of *West Sumatra* (7.5m). Perhaps only 200 Christians. The New Testament was legally published in 1997 but all known copies were burned by West Sumatran authorities

13.5m *Madura* (E Java), 3.8m *Bugis* (S Sulawesi), 3m *Aceh* (N Sumatra)

Many nations will be joined with the Lord in that day and will become my people. Zechariah 2:11

Spain (Western Europe)

o o o o o o o o o o o o o o o

Catholic Church in crisis: over 30% of population, though baptized Catholic, no longer claim any link with Catholicism A further 40-50% are nominal. Charismatic movement small

Spiritual vacuum being filled

by materialism, cults, the occult, drugs, gambling

Evangelical growth has been slow ... 13 million people live in towns, villages or districts where there is no evangelical church. Few of the one million students have had the gospel explained to them.

Qatar (Arab world)

○ ○ ○ ○ ○ ○ ○ ○ ○ ○ ○ ○ ○ ○ ○

No Qatari believers before 1985. Since then, several people have come to the Lord outside the country, but have suffered much for Him

Pray that they may become the nucleus of the Qatari Church

Pray that the small groups of believers among expatriates may bear fruitful witness

If I am to go on living in the body, this will mean fruitful labour for me. Philippians 1:22

Colombia (Latin America)

○ ○ ○ ○ ○ ○ ○ ○ ○ ○ ○ ○ ○ ○ ○

The Church
is growing
rapidly

in a climate of crime, lawlessness, terror, and murder.

Evangelicals grew to nearly 5% in 2000, and Charismatics now number an estimated 17% of the population. This growth is all the more miraculous considering that Christians are often targets of drug cartels, guerrillas, paramilitaries, and others.

As sin increases in Colombia,

God's grace increases all the more

My grace is sufficient for you, for my power is made perfect in weakness. 2 Corinthians 12:9

Children of War

One million children are suffering from chronic malnutrition and 300,000 died from sanctions-related causes in the 1990s *(Iraq)*... All 1.4m children under 17 have been traumatized, have lost their education and many have been orphaned. In 1996 there were still 15,000 carrying guns *(Liberia)* ... **Thousands have been kidnapped, drugged and forced to kill their own relatives *(Sierra Leone)*...** Many Tamil children have been brainwashed into becoming killing machines *(Sri Lanka)*...

The Lord's Resistance Army has abducted over 10,000 children as

child-soldiers or

sex-slaves *(Uganda)*

'... for the kingdom of heaven belongs to such as these.'
Matthew 19:14

Mali and Niger (West Africa)

o o o o o o o o o o o o o o o

Subsistence agricultural desert economies

Mali: Still a pioneer country – less than 2% are Christians. The ecological crisis of the Sahel has brought much help from Christian missions and aid organizations. Protestants and Catholics have grown slowly but steadily.

Significant numbers of converts from a Muslim background

Niger: This Muslim land is open for the gospel, and the loving ministry of Christian aid missionaries has won credibility for the gospel. Yet response has been small and church growth slow.

I know that the LORD secures justice for the poor and upholds the cause of the needy. Psalm 140:12

China – cults and sects

○ ○ ○ ○ ○ ○ ○ ○ ○ ○ ○ ○ ○ ○ ○

Lack of Bible knowledge and of mature leadership has opened the way for many exotic messianic, syncretistic and divisive groups, some of which have spread over much of China. In some areas they now constitute 5% or more of the unregistered church population.

Pray that this growth might be slowed by the loving proclamation of the truth of God's Word through radio, literature and preaching

DAY 73

See to it that no one takes you captive through hollow and deceptive philosophy, which depends on human tradition and the basic principles of this world rather than on Christ. Colossians 2:8

Australia

○ ○ ○ ○ ○ ○ ○ ○ ○ ○ ○ ○ ○ ○ ○

A rapid increase of those claiming no religion

Church attendance declined steadily,

but appears to have stabilized with about 10% of Australians in church on an average Sunday, and 18-20% in regular contact with church life.

Less-reached minorities: Muslims, Chinese, Vietnamese, Jews, peoples from the former Yugoslavia and Southern Europe.

Reconciliation between black and white Australians is a

crucial issue yet to be resolved

O God, do not keep silent; be not quiet, O God, be not still.
Psalm 83:1

Punjab (India)

○ ○ ○ ○ ○ ○ ○ ○ ○ ○ ○ ○ ○ ○ ○

The Punjab is the home state of the Sikhs. A violent guerrilla war waged by Sikh extremists seeking independence led to 25,000 deaths. Praise God that peace came in 1992.

This was followed by rapid economic progress,
healing of inter-communal wounds and

unprecedented openness
for the gospel

There are 25 million Sikhs in the world
Little specific Christian study of and dialogue
with Sikhs has ever really been undertaken.

DAY 74

Benin and Togo (West Africa)

O O O O O O O O O O O O O O O

Benin: Africa's highest percentage of followers of traditional religions (48%).

Church growth is occurring in all regions.

The 1990s may well be seen as the decade of breakthrough for church growth. The president is a born-again Christian.

Togo: A decade of rapid church growth.

Power struggle between president and new transitional government … anarchy and virtual civil war … idolatry, secret societies, growing strength of Islam.

Great is our Lord and mighty in power. Psalm 145:5

Guatemala (Latin America)

O O O O O O O O O O O O O O O

Just 2% of the population owns 80% of the land, marginalizing and oppressing the largely Maya majority

Pray for evangelical leaders from both Mayan and Spanish-speaking communities as they work toward the healing of the nation

The authorities show growing appreciation for Evangelical-inspired solutions to social problems

Pray that unity among Evangelical leaders might continue

DAY 75

If God is for us, who can be against us? Romans 8:31

Myanmar (Southeast Asia)

○ ○ ○ ○ ○ ○ ○ ○ ○ ○ ○ ○ ○ ○

Rich in natural resources, but ravaged by the greed of its rulers

The military regime has turned Myanmar into a prison …
killings, forced labour, rape and imprisonment … Also
seeking to marginalize and even eliminate the Church

Yet church growth continues, mostly among ethnic minorities

Here is my servant … I will put my Spirit on him and he will bring
justice to the nations. Isaiah 42:1

Amerindians (Latin America)

O   O   O   O   O   O   O   O   O   O   O   O   O   O   O

Have long been marginalized, exploited and demeaned, their cultures ravaged by the majority **(Argentina)** … Their treatment in the 20th century has been horrific **(El Salvador)** … Protective laws for the remaining small tribal groups are rarely applied, their cultures are disintegrating **(Brazil)** … Have won significant concessions to preserve their endangered habitat and cultures **(Honduras)** … Many have become Christians **(Paraguay)** …The impact of the gospel on sections of the Quichua is a modern-day miracle **(Ecuador)**

Austria (Europe)

O O O O O O O O O O O O O O O O

Austria is Catholic by culture, not commitment.
An estimated 80% have had dealings with the occult.

The high suicide, abortion and alcoholism statistics indicate

the spiritual need

Freedom of religion was restricted by new legislation in
1998. This has impacted all evangelical groups.

Turkmenistan (Central Asia)

O   O   O   O   O   O   O   O   O   O   O   O   O   O   O

Former Communist leader transformed himself into nationalist dictator. Any opposition is ruthlessly crushed, but the oil-hungry West does not protest.

Ethnic Turkmen Christians increased from one or two to 500-600 in ten years

Hostility

against any evangelical Christian presence has increased since 1997

DAY 77

Have mercy on me, O Lord, for I call to you all day long. Psalm 86:3

Peru (Latin America)

○ ○ ○ ○ ○ ○ ○ ○ ○ ○ ○ ○ ○ ○ ○

National Prayer Movement launched in 1989
in response to 15 years of guerrilla warfare

The results: capture of terrorist leaders in 1992 and 1993

massive turning to Christ

especially among the Quechua of the Andes

Tentative economic recovery … a fragile peace…
Peru needs an effective government

**Lima, the capital, is Latin
America's fifth-largest city.
Over 60% live in slums
… abject poverty,
unemployment,
malnutrition**

Call on his name; make known among the nations what he has done.
1 Chronicles 16:8

Bengali people

○ ○ ○ ○ ○ ○ ○ ○ ○ ○ ○ ○ ○ ○ ○

By **far** the largest unreached people in the world with a global total of over 230 million

The majority live in Bangladesh and India, but large communities live in Britain, USA and elsewhere

William Carey went to the Bengali as a missionary. Although they revere Carey's memory, the great breakthrough has still not come after 200 years

Now could be the time for the Bengali people!

Many are torn between being good Bengali and good Muslims

DAY 78

USA

o o o o o o o o o o o o o o o o

The USA's role in the 1990s has been unique as the sole superpower. Globalization is largely driven by US technology, media and culture

The Christian Church is not impacting the nation as it should

Prayer challenges: biblical holiness; commitment to the Bible; spiritual unity; withdrawal from, or involvement in, public life; young people (the next generation could be America's most traumatized ever); the Afro-American community; the Native Americans/First Nations; the 1.8 million prison population

Pray that the events surrounding

September 11, 2001

may be used by God as a wake-up call to the entire Church and nation with long-term positive outcomes

USA

O O O O O O O O O O O O O O O

Prayer networks increased significantly in the 1990s …
Massive growth of the newer Pentecostal and, even more, the
charismatic networks … Localized revivals with

thousands repenting

A strong movement against the evils of society …
Dynamic networks of congregations have sprung up among
Koreans (3,000 churches), Chinese, Filipinos, Arabs and even
Iranians … **Student ministries have flourished …**
The US contribution to world evangelization is unique

DAY 79

We pray … that you may live a life worthy of the Lord and may
please him in every way: bearing fruit in every good work, growing
in the knowledge of God. Colossians 1:10

Burkina Faso (West Africa)

○ ○ ○ ○ ○ ○ ○ ○ ○ ○ ○ ○ ○ ○

One of the world's poorest countries

Over 80% of the population relies on subsistence agriculture

Significant

people movements with thousands of conversions but 24 peoples are still without an effective witness. The power of the occult has yet to be decisively challenged and broken in many peoples.

See, I am doing a new thing! Now it springs up; do you not perceive it? I am making a way in the desert and streams in the wasteland.
Isaiah 43:19

China's ethnic minorities

○ ○ ○ ○ ○ ○ ○ ○ ○ ○ ○ ○ ○ ○ ○

- 100 million people in 464 ethnic groups
- 368 peoples are less than 1% Christian
- 25m people in these ethnic groups are Muslims: Uyghur, Kazak, Uzbek, Kyrgyz, Tajik, Tatar, Hui

Islam is a sensitive issue because of a past history of revolts and unrest. Few Chinese believers feel adequately prepared for outreach

Pray for the gospel to reach these peoples and for committed workers to go to them

DAY 80

The harvest is plentiful, but the workers are few. Luke 10:2

Czech Republic and Slovakia
(Eastern Europe)

O O O O O O O O O O O O O O

The bloodless 'velvet revolution' against Communist rule in 1989 was followed by rapid democratization and the 'velvet divorce' that created the two nations in 1993.

Czech Republic: Influence of the Church is fading rapidly … an increase in crime, substance abuse, prostitution and

family breakdown

Pray that this negative spiral might be cut short by the intervention of God

Evangelical churches growing

Slovakia: Strong Christian heritage but Catholic and mainline Protestant churches are declining. Evangelical denominations few and small.

You heavens above, rain down righteousness; let the clouds shower it down. Isaiah 45:8

United Arab Emirates (Arab world)

○ ○ ○ ○ ○ ○ ○ ○ ○ ○ ○ ○ ○ ○ ○

Radical changes in the last generation have made UAE citizens more cosmopolitan and open to new ideas, yet the rise of extreme Islamism has led to increased restrictions

Many people are in daily contact with Christians, but few believers have opportunity to share their faith because of the possible results - arrests are not unusual

There are some Gulf Arab believers
Their faith exposes them to

persecution and

possibly even *death*

DAY 81

But God's word is not chained. 2 Timothy 2:9

Brunei (Southeast Asia)

○ ○ ○ ○ ○ ○ ○ ○ ○ ○ ○ ○ ○ ○ ○ ○

One of the richest states in Asia. Oil is the sole source of wealth and reserves may be used up by 2020. The Sultan rules as an absolute monarch. Islam is the state religion.

Limitations
on Christian activity are increasing

Who is it that overcomes the world? Only he who believes that Jesus is the Son of God. 1 John 5:5

Orissa (India)

○ ○ ○ ○ ○ ○ ○ ○ ○ ○ ○ ○ ○ ○ ○
38 million people   2.1% Christian

Persecution of Christians increased during the 1990s.
Orissa shares with Gujarat the worst record for Hindu
extremist violence. Many churches have been destroyed
and Christian workers attacked, some molested and killed

Church growth
also increased

in the 1990s despite harsh state
anti-conversion laws

**Blessed are those who are persecuted because of righteousness,
for theirs is the kingdom of heaven.** Matthew 5:10

Germany's rapid spiritual decline might be slowing: **there is**

increased

enthusiasm

among young people for spiritual things and evangelical and charismatic churches are growing.

Germany's wealth, power and strategic location in Europe could be of great value for the Kingdom of God. For this, a strong, courageous leadership based on Christian values is needed.

Ghana (West Africa)

O O O O O O O O O O O O O O O

There has been a spiritual upsurge

The evangelistic zeal of many churches and
agencies has brought thousands to new life.
Also, a big increase in evangelism among
the animistic and Muslim northern peoples.

Rapid growth of African Independent churches which
offer excitement, involvement and miracles, but not always
salvation by faith

Pray that the true gospel may shine into hearts

My soul finds rest in God alone; my salvation comes from him.
He alone is my rock and my salvation; he is my fortress,
I will never be shaken. Psalm 62:1,2

Russia

A proud but despairing nation …

Poverty, hopelessness, crime, drug abuse, family breakdown, suicide. 30% live on less than US$1/day; 1.2 million street children; 650,000 orphans in grim orphanages and prisons; 40% of men are alcoholics

Up to 100 ethnic minorities without a church or at a pioneer stage
The North Caucasus peoples – in Dagestan and Chechnya for example – are some of the least-reached on earth

*Pray for open doors
to these people*

Russia's Church

○ ○ ○ ○ ○ ○ ○ ○ ○ ○ ○ ○ ○ ○ ○

Communism's collapse with little bloodshed was a direct answer to prayer. Churches of all kinds doubled to 15,000 in the 1990s. Roman Catholics multiplied

The Orthodox Church is using every possible means to regain its exclusive spiritual dominance

Evangelical congregations increased, but the expected harvest was not brought in. *To blame?*
Inappropriate evangelism; serious divisions; the need for practical holiness; emigration of Christians

Over 90% of Russians have no meaningful link with any church

In the LORD alone are righteousness and strength. Isaiah 45:24

DAY 84

Côte d'Ivoire (West Africa)

O O O O O O O O O O O O O O O

One of the world's largest producers of cocoa, coffee
and palm oil. Ivorian stability is essential to the entire region.

Rapid growth in evangelical churches, and the charismatic movement is well established in the Catholic Church

700 Protestant/Independent churches in **Abidjan**, the largest city
Abidjan is the key for the evangelization of Côte d' Ivoire,
Mali and Burkina Faso. Every people of these lands has a significant
community in the city. Most are neglected by the Church.

Northeast Indian States – selected

○ ○ ○ ○ ○ ○ ○ ○ ○ ○ ○ ○ ○ ○ ○

Mizoram is one of the most active Christian states in the world. Awakenings and revivals in recent years have dynamized the Church and transformed society. Over 2,000 Mizo missionaries in India and beyond

Nagaland: Thousands have served the Lord in other parts of India and beyond. But Christian witness is compromised by feuding, corruption, denominational fragmentation

growing nominalism

Manipur: Denominational and ethnic conflicts severely

hamper outreach

DAY 85

May the God who gives endurance and encouragement give you a spirit of unity among yourselves as you follow Christ Jesus. Romans 15:5

Cuba (Caribbean)

○ ○ ○ ○ ○ ○ ○ ○ ○ ○ ○ ○ ○ ○ ○

The void created by Communism is being
filled by Christianity:

- A rally in Havana, which Castro himself attended, drew 100,000 Christians
- Castro's own son is an active believer
- There are 4,500 congregations and a further 10,000 house groups in 54 denominations

A high proportion of the new Christians are young people

Pray that the growth may continue whatever the political situation

But I pray to you, O Lord, in the time of your favour; in your great love, O God, answer me with your sure salvation. Psalm 69:13

Oman (Arab world)

○ ○ ○ ○ ○ ○ ○ ○ ○ ○ ○ ○ ○ ○

The entire Muslim majority is a **big** challenge

There are perhaps a handful of indigenous believers, none professing Christ openly

Almost the entire Christian population is expatriate. Churches are very active

Pray for the Christians to live godly lives that clearly display Christ to their neighbours

DAY 86

Liberia and Sierra Leone (West Africa)

Liberia: Founded as a Christian state but for decades Christians compromised with evil on an alarming scale. The 1989 revolution engulfed the country in an orgy of inter-tribal killings. Relative peace since 1996.

The *agony* of the nation has driven Christians to new prayer and earnestness for the gospel

Sierra Leone: The Liberian civil war triggered the collapse of the government. Now it is probably the poorest and most desperate country on earth. Anarchy reigns.

Those who hope in the Lord will renew their strength. Isaiah 40:31

Netherlands, Belgium, Luxembourg

O O O O O O O O O O O O O O O

Netherlands: A great history as a Christian nation
A dramatic decline in the number of Christians in this
generation. Today's openly permissive society is

renouncing its heritage

Belgium: The population is culturally Catholic but rapidly
secularizing. Protestantism has hardly grown over the past
30 years

Luxembourg: While the vast majority profess Catholicism,
only a shrinking fraction actively practice their faith. Many
Catholics dabble in Buddhism and the New Age

DAY 87

Why should the nations say, 'Where is their God?' Psalm 79:10

Venezuela (Latin America)

○ ○ ○ ○ ○ ○ ○ ○ ○ ○ ○ ○ ○ ○ ○

Poverty is widespread, living standards are plummeting
(60% of urbanites live in slums) and crime is soaring

Majority of Catholics are nominal. Up to 85% of the
population are involved in spiritism

Tremendous

evangelical growth

in the last decade. Evangelical believers grew
from one million in 1990 to around 2.5m in 2000

As many as 50,000 people lost their lives in floods and
landslides in 2000, and about 400,000 were made homeless

You hear, O Lord, the desire of the afflicted; you encourage them,
and you listen to their cry. Psalm 10:17

China's Three Self Churches

○ ○ ○ ○ ○ ○ ○ ○ ○ ○ ○ ○ ○ ○ ○

Three Self Patriotic Movement churches were started by 'patriotic' and often theologically liberal Christians with the strong encouragement of the Communist Party. Restrictions include: no youth work, a ban on healing, and limited evangelism

Praise God for many who quietly ignore the rules

Growth is dramatic:
**500,000 baptisms in the TSPM churches every year
Adult membership in 1997 was estimated at**
17 million

Cambodia (Southeast Asia)

O O O O O O O O O O O O O O O

Major economic activities:
- Receiving international aid
- Sin (pornography, prostitution, drugs and illegal logging)

The terrible genocide of 1975-79 in which nearly 2 million were killed has left deep physical and emotional scars

The spiritual darkness of Cambodia
must be lifted by prayer

The Cambodian Church has survived against all the odds: there were 300 evangelical congregations in 1999, with more than one new church starting each week – almost entirely through local people

Guinea (West Africa)

○ ○ ○ ○ ○ ○ ○ ○ ○ ○ ○ ○ ○ ○ ○ ○

The Christian population is still a small minority

Pray that the Holy Spirit will transform individuals, families and tribes, making them models for a truly African Christian lifestyle

Most peoples are still a pioneer challenge

There is a growing expectancy among believers for an abundant harvest

DAY 89

In the morning, O Lord, you hear my voice; in the morning I lay my requests before you and wait in expectation. Psalm 5:3

Romania (Eastern Europe)

O O O O O O O O O O O O O O O

- Lags ever further behind other former Communist states
- Vacuum left by Communism has been replaced by every kind of social evil: substance abuse, prostitution, violent crime, abortion

Hundreds of thousands of orphans and street children

- Church has developed well with good foundations for future leadership. But also: legalism, isolation, ethnic divisions, and materialism
- Minority Christian groups are persecuted by the Orthodox Church

A bruised reed he will not break, and a smoldering wick he will not snuff out. Isaiah 42:3

New world-missions movements

O O O O O O O O O O O O O O O

Nearly 500 **Japanese** missionaries have been or are serving overseas … A number of **Argentineans** are internationally respected mission leaders … 2,000 cross-cultural **Brazilian** missionaries are serving in 92 agencies and 85 nations … **Nigeria** has become one of the major missionary-sending countries with 3,700 cross-cultural workers … **Korea** now has 8,000 missionaries serving in other lands …
Dynamic growth surge of **Indian** mission initiatives: 44,000 cross-cultural workers (mostly within India) in 2000

They will proclaim my glory among the nations. And they will bring all your brothers, from all the nations, to my holy mountain.
Isaiah 66:19-20

Bolivia (Latin America)

○ ○ ○ ○ ○ ○ ○ ○ ○ ○ ○ ○ ○ ○ ○

Spiritual darkness of centuries
beginning to be broken, but

Christians

need

to grapple
in prayer

with the entrenched idolatry,
pagan superstitions, injustices,
corruption and vested interests
of those with power

. . . His incomparably great power for us who believe . . .
Ephesians 1:19

Small African countries

○ ○ ○ ○ ○ ○ ○ ○ ○ ○ ○ ○ ○ ○ ○ ○

Cape Verde Islands (West Africa)
Caboverdians are Christian in name (93% Catholic),
but in practice are more influenced by superstitions

Guinea-Bissau (West Africa)
43% Muslim; 41% Traditional; 14% Christian (mostly
Catholic). One of the poorest countries in the world
Over 27 ethnic groups

*Pray that the national church might
receive the courage and gifts to reach
out to unreached groups with the gospel*

São Tomé and Principé (West Africa)
Vast majority are Catholic but
ninety percent of children are
born illegitimately

Haryana and Rajasthan (India)

Haryana: 20 million people, only 500 churches
Only 15 of the 92 people groups have any congregations

Rajasthan: 53 million people; 0.12% Christian

Pray for the continued

increase

in workers and churches

despite anti-conversion laws and rising opposition

Answer me quickly, O LORD; my spirit fails. Psalm 143:7

Estonia, Latvia, Lithuania
(Eastern Europe)

O O O O O O O O O O O O O O O

The Church is now free!

Estonia: Nominalism is widespread in an ageing Lutheran State Church

Latvia: Only about 2% of the population regularly attend church. Smaller evangelical denominations grow, the Lutheran and Catholic churches struggle

Lithuania: The Catholic Church plays a key role. Religious freedom has stimulated growth, in particular newer groups of charismatics and Pentecostals

DAY 92

In him and through faith in him we may approach God with freedom and confidence. Ephesians 3:12

Tajikistan (Central Asia)

○ ○ ○ ○ ○ ○ ○ ○ ○ ○ ○ ○ ○ ○ ○

Mountainous former Soviet state
Fifty thousand killed in civil war which ended in 1997

Poverty and extreme hardship common

Open for sensitive Christian ministry

Small, growing Church

**Hundreds of believers in Tajikistan, a further 1000+
Tajik believers in Afghanistan, Pakistan, Uzbekistan**

For Christ died for sins once for all, the righteous for
the unrighteous, to bring you to God. 1 Peter 3:18

Senegal and Gambia (West Africa)

○ ○ ○ ○ ○ ○ ○ ○ ○ ○ ○ ○ ○ ○ ○

Subsistence agriculture, many ethnic groups

Senegal: Islam grew to 92% by 2000. Most Muslims belong to one of three powerful Sufi brotherhoods

Praise God for religious freedom

Evangelical believers are few, the rate of growth slow. Only now are stable congregations emerging after years of work

Gambia: 25 ethnic groups among 1.3 million people. Little effort has ever been directed at reaching the Muslim majority

Pray for continued freedom to witness and for openness of heart in Muslims

Yemen (Arab world)

O O O O O O O O O O O O O O

Deeply impacted by wars …
over 50 million firearms in the country

Illegal for Muslims to become Christians. Yet through radio
broadcasts, tactful faith-sharing and the Lord's intervention
perhaps 100 or so Yemenis have trusted in Christ

Widening range
of opportunities

for expatriates to serve the Lord in business,
education, health and development programmes

For as … a garden causes seeds to grow, so the Sovereign Lord will
make righteousness and praise spring up before all nations. Isaiah 61:11

Renewal within Catholicism

Catholic charismatic renewal has had an impact far beyond the 100 million or so who are, or have been, involved. A large proportion of the Catholic missionary force is charismatic. The Evangelical Catholic movement has been gaining in

influence and numbers

with its more biblical interpretation of faith

Pray that millions of nominal Catholics may come to a warm, living faith in the Lord Jesus, and not lose their spiritual dynamism by being absorbed and neutralized by the system

DAY 94

The LORD your God . . . is mighty to save. Zephaniah 3:17

Maldive Islands (South Asia)
Comoros Islands (East Africa)

○ ○ ○ ○ ○ ○ ○ ○ ○ ○ ○ ○ ○ ○ ○ ○

Maldive Islands

No Christian mission work has ever been permitted

Yet some Maldivians came to faith during the 1990s. A severe crack-down by the authorities in 1998 … the imprisonment and torture of 50 Maldivians suspected of being Christian.

Comoros Islands: All open witness is forbidden in this Islamic state … no official Comoran churches.

His rule will extend far from sea to sea. Zechariah 9:13

HIV & AIDS

14% known to be HIV+ and 310,000 AIDS orphans (**Mozambique**) ... Life expectancy cut to 43 and up to 400,000 orphans (**Malawi**) ... 14% infected and 730,000 orphans (**Kenya**) ... 1.4 m AIDS orphans (**Nigeria**) ... 30-35% of the population infected (**Botswana**) ... Orphans from genocide, war and AIDS may number 500,000 (**Rwanda**) ... 420,000 AIDS orphans (**South Africa**) ... 1.1 m orphaned children (**Tanzania**) ... Infection rate is falling; 2m orphans (**Uganda**) ... 20-25% infected and 650,000 AIDS orphans. Extended families too over-stretched to care for them all (**Zambia**) ... 1 m orphans, 9% of the population (**Zimbabwe**)

Is anything too hard for the LORD? Genesis 18:14

DAY 95

Iran

○ ○ ○ ○ ○ ○ ○ ○ ○ ○ ○ ○ ○ ○ ○ ○

The Islamic revolution has lost its glitter. The legacy of
bloodshed, cruelty, injustice,

extremism and economic deprivation has discredited the
conservative religious leaders and the Islam they promote

The number of Muslim-background Christians has multiplied in 20 years
Estimates range from 4,000 to 20,000 with half in Iran and half overseas

Persecution
is too severe
to uncover
the true
situation

And will not God bring about justice for his chosen ones, who cry
out to him day and night? Will he keep putting them off? I tell you,
he will see that they get justice, and quickly. Luke 18:7-8

Drugs

O O O O O O O O O O O O O O O

About 50% of the world's cocaine is grown in *Bolivia*

Pray that Bolivian Evangelicals may live holy, exemplary lives as they seek to bring change

Over 200,000 rural *Peruvians* are involved in cultivating narcotics

The most successful export is opium *(Myanmar)* Opium poppies are the only lucrative cash crop for most of the northern tribes. Cultivation is an acute temptation for Christians *(Thailand)*

DAY 96

Albania (Eastern Europe)

○ ○ ○ ○ ○ ○ ○ ○ ○ ○ ○ ○ ○ ○

One of Europe's poorest countries

Communism has been economically, morally and spiritually devastating

Over one million Qur'ans have been distributed, 900 mosques refurbished or built between 1993 and 1995

The evangelical witness in Albania has grown dramatically since 1991 By 2000 there were over 130 congregations, one in every city or town

Pray for peace and that ethnic and religious hatreds may not erode the present freedoms

Mauritania (West Africa)

O O O O O O O O O O O O O O O O O

One of the world's poorest countries
One third of children are malnourished

Harsh climate (sandstorms 200 days a year)

Officially an Islamic Republic

The government takes great pains to keep Christianity away from the people. Individuals showing interest in Christianity in the past have been *imprisoned or tortured*

DAY 97

But this is a people plundered and looted, all of them trapped in pits or hidden away in prisons. They have become plunder, with no one to rescue them. Isaiah 42:22

Afghanistan (Central Asia)

○ ○ ○ ○ ○ ○ ○ ○ ○ ○ ○ ○ ○ ○ ○ ○

Pray that the unprecedented openness to the gospel may ultimately lead to a great harvest. Pray for a just, fair and honourable government to be raised up

Ecological disaster, over 12 million uncleared anti-personnel mines and the capital in ruins

48,000 mosques, but not a single church building

Pray for the 70 unreached peoples of this land

All the nations you have made will come and worship before you, O LORD; they will bring glory to your name. Psalm 86:9

African Independent Churches

○ ○ ○ ○ ○ ○ ○ ○ ○ ○ ○ ○ ○ ○ ○ ○

Maybe thousands of denominations – ranging from an evangelical theological position to a high degree of compromise with polygamy, witchcraft, ancestor veneration and appeasement sacrifices

Massive growth:

10% of all Africans belong at least loosely to independent churches

Pray that this extraordinary and significant movement may retain the best of African culture yet become biblical and accountable to the wider Body of Christ

DAY 98

Saudi Arabia (Arab world)

○ ○ ○ ○ ○ ○ ○ ○ ○ ○ ○ ○ ○ ○ ○

An Islamic state, custodian of Islam

Probably the world's worst record on religious freedom and human rights

Saudis who confess Christ face the death penalty

Still, a growing and substantial
number are secretly seeking
and finding
Him

He will not falter or be discouraged till he establishes justice on the earth. Isaiah 42:4

Jewish Christians

Globally there has been a significant response to Christ among the 15 million Jews; around 132,000 are linked with Messianic congregations (which retain Jewish cultural distinctives) and a further 200,000 with Gentile churches

In Israel: Messianic Jews have increased from 250 in 1967 to possibly 7,000 in 2000. They are denied legal standing as a religious body

But the LORD will be a refuge for his people. Joel 3:16

Uttar Pradesh and Uttaranchal (India)

o o o o o o o o o o o o o

173 million people in these two North Indian states. The Christian Church has long been a tiny, stagnant minority community of 230,000 people; 80-90% nominal

The awesome immensity of the unfinished task …

Let us fix our eyes on Jesus, the author and perfecter of our faith, who for the joy set before him endured the cross, scorning its shame, and sat down at the right hand of the throne of God.
Hebrew 12:2

China's house churches

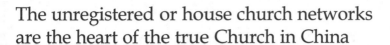

The unregistered or house church networks are the heart of the true Church in China

Intense persecution has indigenized and purified it

Prayer, revival, simple living

and a Christocentric theology characterize it

Twenty or more larger networks exist

Estimates count between
30 and 80 million people

belonging to the unregistered churches

DAY 100

'In the last days,' God says, 'I will pour out my Spirit on all people.' Acts 2:17

100 days

O O O O O O O O O O O O O O O

Operation World research and original text:
Patrick Johnstone, Jason Mandryk and
Robyn Johnstone

100 days compiler: Glenn Myers

Design and supplementary material:
Dave Davidson and Glenn Myers
Special thanks to:
Daphne Spraggett and Peter Little

www.operationworld.org

100 Days (8507.8428) – Trade Offer

Use this voucher to reclaim the cost of this book, £4.99, when purchasing either Operation World or Window On The World.

Name of Customer...

Address...

....

To the Retailer: This completed voucher entitles the bearer to a discount of £4.99 against the purchase of either Operation World 1-85078-357-9 (RRP £14.99) or Window On The World 1-85078-358-6 (RRP £14.99). Vouchers will be credited less normal discount. Please return the voucher to: STL Customer Services, PO Box 300, Carlisle, CA3 0QS, by 30/09/2002.

Name of
Retailer...
STL A/c No..

Only one voucher to be used per customer. Voucher cannot be used in conjunction with any other offer. Voucher cannot be exchanged for anything other than the above products. No change will be given. Cash Value 0.0001p. Offer expires 30/09.2002. Code

100 Days (8507.8428) – Direct Offer

SAVE £4.99. Use this voucher to reclaim the cost of this book when purchasing either Operation World or Window On The World from Wesley Owen Direct, PO Box 19, Carlisle, CA3 0HP. PAY BY CHEQUE OR CREDIT CARD. Please indicate which book you wish to order:

Operation World (8507.8357) RRP £14.99 Offer Price £10 ☐

Window On The World (8507.8358) RRP £14.99 Offer Price £10 ☐

I enclose a Cheque for £12.95 (including £2.95 UK P&P) payable to Wesley Owen Direct

Name..

Address...

....**Postcode**...................................

Telephone number...

Please charge my Visa/Mastercard/Switch

Please note we are unable to accept Switch Solo cards or American Express cards

Name on card..

Cardholder's signature...

Card Number...

Start Date...........................**Expiry Date**..

Switch Issue Number...

Cardholder's address (if different)...

....

Postcode..

Email..

Only one voucher to be used per customer. Voucher cannot be used in conjunction with any other offer. Voucher cannot be exchanged for anything other than the above products. No change will be given. Cash Value 0.0001p. Offer expires 30/09/2002.